Cardboard Dad

By **Alan Harris**

This play was produced by Sherman Cymru and first performed at Sherman, Cardiff, on Thursday 15 October, 2009.

Alan Harris asserts his moral right to be identified as the author of this work.

Cover Image: Kirsten McTernan
Design: Rhys Huws
Typesetting: Eira Fenn

Printed in Wales by Cambrian Printers, Aberystwyth. This book is published with the financial support of the Welsh Books Council.

ISBN: 0-9551466-9-0   978-0-955146-9-5

   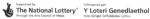

CAST

Shelley Rees
Simon Nehan

PRODUCTION TEAM

Writer	Alan Harris
Director	Juliet Knight
Designer	Joanna Scotcher
Lighting Designer	Ace McCarron
Sound Designer	Becky Smith
Choreographer	David Grewcock
Music Arrangement for	Arwyn Davies
Feeling Good	
Stage Manager	Natasha White
Deputy Stage Manager	Elaine Yeung
Set Construction	Mathew Thomas & Abe Ahmed

THANKS

Theatr Iolo; Haleh Tozer

SHERMAN CYMRU

We aim to make and present great theatre that is ambitious, inventive and memorable for our audiences, and to create strong, responsive and enriching relationships with our communities. We strive to create the best theatre we can; to achieve a distinct and diverse programme for our audiences; to engage our communities in the creative process of theatre making; and to make a lasting contribution to the national and international development of theatre in Wales. We produce work in both English and Welsh, and tour widely within Wales and the UK.

To be kept in touch about Sherman Cymru events register for our e-bulletin online at **www.shermancymru.co.uk**

Capital Newsflash......

If you haven't already heard our news then we're delighted to let you know that we have secured a £3.9m Lottery grant from the Arts Council of Wales to enable us to move ahead with a redevelopment of Sherman. This major project will enhance your enjoyment every time you visit and provide us with a much better work environment.

There will be a variety of ways for you to help us raise the remaining £1.5 million that we need to make these exciting changes a reality. You can now make a £2 contribution to the campaign when you book your tickets to see a show, either at our box office, over the phone or online. To keep informed about our campaign activities you can register for our e-bulletins – **www.shermancymru.co.uk/register** or if you are already on our e-list you can log in to your account to select Campaign Updates in your newsletter preferences.

Sherman Cymru acknowledges the public investment of the Arts Council of Wales and Cardiff Council without whose support our work could not continue. Our Learning and Engagement work is currently supported by Paul Hamlyn Foundation and The Rayne Foundation. Recent productions and projects have also been supported by Barclays, Arts & Business Cymru, Esmée Fairbairn Foundation, Oakdale Trust and The Peggy Ramsay Foundation.

v

Shelley Rees
Donna

Theatre
Burberry (Sherman Cymru
SpringBoard:Egin Festival); *The Gut
Girls* (Velvet Ensemble); *Pulling the
Wool, Bedside Manners* (Sherman
Theatre Company); *House of
America* (Fiction Factory); *Y
Groesffordd* (Dalier Sylw); *In Sunshine
and In Shadow* (Merthyr Inc.).

Television
Dau Dŷ a Ni, Eros Unleashed (ITV
Wales); *Uncle Mike, Pobol y Cwm,
Belonging* (BBC Television); *Jones,
Jones, Jones* (Cwmni Da); *Nuts
and Bolts, Glan Hafren* (HTV); *Y
Glas, Iechyd Da* (S4C); *Mind to Kill*
(Lluniau Lliw/Yorkshire TV). Shelley
was recently nominated for the Bafta
Cymru Best Actress award for her
role as Joanna Pugh in *Dau Dŷ a Ni*.

Film
Good Arrows (Dust Films); *31/12/99*
(Bracan); *Provence, Gadael Lenin*
(Gaucho Films); *Cwm Hyfryd*
(Millennium Films).

Radio
Jack, Farblas (BBC Radio 4).

Shelley is also an experienced
voiceover artist and sings with the
rock group, The Amendments.

Simon Nehan
David

Simon trained at the Royal Welsh
College of Music and Drama. He
is an Associate Artist at Clwyd
Theatr Cymru.

Theatre
*Noises Off, Macbeth, Two Princes,
Grapes of Wrath, The Druid's Rest, A
Portrait of the Artist as a Young Dog,
Mabinogi, Silas Marner, The Rabbit,
Hosts of Rebecca, Rape of the Fair
Country, Song of the Earth* (Clwyd
Theatr Cymru); *Memory* (Clwyd
Theatr Cymru/59E59 Theatre, New
York); *Acqua Nero* (Sgript Cymru);
The Canterbury Tales, As You Like It
(Mappa Mundi); *The Seagull, Kebab
Shags* (Bristol Old Vic); *A Child's
Christmas In Wales* (Theatr na n'Og);
Stella Time (Antic Theatre).

Television
*Holby City, Casualty, First Degree,
Stopping Distance, The Bench, Score,
Kardomah Boys* (BBC Television);
Merlin II (BBC/Shine); *Nuts And
Bolts, The Comedy Show* (HTV
Wales).

Film
Dagenham Girls (Number 9 Films);
The Shouting Men (Away Days); *Me
and Orson Welles* (CinemaNX/Fuzzy
Bunny); *Tracy Beaker - Movie Of Me*
(BBC Television).

Alan Harris
Writer

Alan's first play, *Orange*, was produced by Sgript Cymru. Other work includes: *Miss Brown To You* (Hijinx Theatre – UK Tour); *Burberry* (Sherman Cymru SpringBoard:Egin Festival); *The Loneliness of the Long Distance Bus Driver* (Paines Plough - performed at Later, Trafalgar Studios, London); *Brute* (The Operating Theatre Company – performed at the Tristan Bates Theatre, London).

He is currently working on commissions for the Welsh National Opera's MAX department (*The Journey*) and BBC Radio 3 (*The Gold Farmer*). He has also worked with Pentabus Theatre and the National Youth Theatre of Great Britain as a writing workshop leader and with WNO MAX on various projects, including *Songlines*, *Song Bus* and *Surf Tailz*, an exploration of the connections between opera and sport that culminated in a surf DVD.

As well as tutoring on the new writers' course at Sherman Cymru, Alan is currently working with prisoners at HMP Cardiff to produce a new radio play, and is developing a new contemporary opera.

Juliet Knight
Director

Juliet trained at Rose Bruford Drama School and started work as an actor. As a director she works primarily on new writing projects, developing texts with writers and actors. She is a co-founder of Talking Pictures Productions.

Works in development for 2010 include: *Razia Sultan* (Tramway Theatre, Glasgow); *Changing Your Story* (Soho Theatre/Clean Break); *A Just Act*, *Welcome Night* (Clean Break).

As director theatre credits include: *DNA*, *It Snows* (Clean Break); *Catch* (Royal Court/Clean Break); *Us or Them* (UK Tour); *White Boy*, *Out of Me*, *Prime Resident* (Soho Theatre/National Youth Theatre); *100 Word Stories*, *Octavia* (Soho Theatre); *Larks in the Park* (Site-specific performance in Richmond Park, London); *A Midsummer Night's Dream* (Assistant Director – Bloomsbury Theatre).

Juliet is also an Associate Director for National Youth Theatre, a Shakespeare Schools Facilitator, a Workshop Leader and an Acting Course Director. She has devised work in Aylesbury and Huntercombe Young Offender Institutes and in Preston Manor PRU.

Joanna Scotcher
Designer

Joanna trained in Theatre Design and completed a graduate design apprenticeship with the Royal Shakespeare Company.

Credits include design assistant on *The Histories Cycle*, *King Lear*, *The Seagull* and *Noughts & Crosses* (Royal Shakespeare Company). Her other design work includes *Inches Apart* (Old Vic New Voices at Theatre 503); *Wagstaffe* (Mercury Theatre); *Paradise* (Sheffield Crucible); *The Spider Men* (National Theatre, Cottesloe); *Wired* (The King's Head Theatre); *Blooded* (New Perspectives Theatre Company) and costume design for *Don Juan Comes Back From the War* (The Belgrade Theatre, Coventry).

In 2008 she received the York Prize for Theatre Design and was commissioned to design *Patient No. 1* (York Theatre Royal) and then a site-specific version of *The Railway Children* at The National Railway Museum.

She is currently attached to the Look Left Look Right Theatre Company, where her work has specialised in promenade and site responsive design. Her design work with them includes *The Caravan* (The Royal Court); *The Roundhouse History* (The Roundhouse) and *Economy* (Battersea Arts Centre).

Ace McCarron
Lighting Designer

Ace has designed lighting for a substantial number of productions for Music Theatre Wales, National Youth Theatre of Wales, Theatr Genedlaethol Cymru, Shared Experience and Paines Plough.

He has been proud of his numerous designs for children's companies, black theatre companies and for the operas of Sir Peter Maxwell Davies.

Recent work includes: *Quadrophenia* (National Tour); *The Snow Queen*, *The Almond and the Seahorse*, *Beauty and the Beast* (Sherman Cymru); *Amadeus*, *The Tailor's Daughter* (John Doyle); *Jasser* (Stichting Bodylab in Rotterdam); *20 Men Singing*, *20 Women Singing*, *A Marvellous Medicine* (Max Department at WNO).

Becky Smith
Sound Designer

Sound designs include: *It Felt Empty*, *Missing Out*, *This Wide Night* (Clean Break); *Frozen* (Fresh Glory); *The Juniper Tree*, *Reverence*, *The Ghost Sonata*, *Visual Hallucinations* (Goat and Monkey); *The Moonslave*, *Johnny Formidable* (Punchdrunk); *Seven* (Arc Theatre).

Becky also works as a Stage Manager and Workshop Leader and has worked with Oily Cart, Paines Plough, Top of the World, Schtanhaus, Polka Theatre, The Comedy School and London Bubble.

Cardboard Dad

By **Alan Harris**

ACT 1

This production was performed using two actors.

A one-bedroom flat.
A typical day for Donna . . .
She enters from the utility room, dustpan and brush in hand.
She sweeps up a mound of debris on the floor and puts it in the
bin.
She takes the dustpan and brush back out to the utility room
and re-enters with the polish. She sprays a bit into the air and
smells it. She polishes.
She goes to the kitchen area and puts on a pinny. She opens
some beans and puts them in a pan and stirs. She puts the TV
on. She presses play on the video player. An aerobics video
comes on. She does some aerobics. She stirs the beans. She gets
two cans and uses them as weights while doing the video. She
stops. She takes off the pinny.
She goes to the bedroom and puts on a hoodie which is too big
for her.
She returns to the living room and takes the radio, a cushion and
a book on to the floor. She tunes in the radio. It's 'Classic FM'.
She turns it up and reads a book while lying on her front. She
rolls over onto her back and reads. On the radio Mendelssohn's
'Wedding March' comes on. It's followed by adverts, one for a
Relaxation CD, and then the news. There is an item about
supporting the troops in Afghanistan. She listens to it then turns
off the radio.
She gets up and sits on the settee. She writes a letter. She folds
the letter and leaves it on the arm of the settee. She gives a
teddy bear, which is on the settee, a hug.
She goes to the bedroom and looks at David's clothes. She
smells them. She does the buttons up on a shirt. She puts on a
dressing gown.
She goes to the kitchen and sits at the table for a while.

1

She gets the letter, takes it to the bedroom and puts it in the pocket of one of David's coats.

She goes to bed. While she is lying there she spins a globe which is at the head of the bed.

She gets up, puts her dressing gown on again, goes to the kitchen and makes a cup of tea. On the way she picks up a notebook from the living room. She does an inventory of food and makes a list of what is needed.

She turns on the computer and does an internet shop.

She puts the notebook back and notices the polish. She takes it to the utility room, giving a spray and sniff on the way.

She goes to the bedroom and takes off the dressing gown.

The doorbell. A knock.

She answers the door. It's the Tesco delivery man. She takes the shopping and puts it in the kitchen. She rifles through the shopping, which is all own-brand goods, and gets out a packet of Jammie Dodgers (originals, not Tesco brand), opens them and eats two.

She takes the bill and sits on the settee. She gets out her notebook. She makes a calculation and writes in the book. She tears out the page and gets out a box. Out of the box she gets a jar. She puts the piece of paper in the jar which is stuffed with similar bits of paper.

She goes to the utility room, and comes back with dustpan and brush in hand. She sweeps up a mound of debris on the floor and puts it in the bin.

She takes the dustpan and brush back out to the utility room and re-enters with the polish. She sprays a bit into the air and smells it. She polishes.

The doorbell.

A knock. A knock.

Again the bell. And a knock.

She answers the door.

– Sign.

2

I never ordered it.

– Your name Donna Wilson?

But/

– Will you sign or not?

If it'll help.

– Only if you're Donna Wilson.

Where do I sign?

– Is this for you?

I've said. No. I never ordered it.

Pause.

But I'll sign.

– What?

If that's easier.

– You never ordered it but you're willing to sign?

If it helps.

– I'm not so sure you should sign now.

Pause.

– Just here.

She comes back in with a large, flat package which has a letter sellotaped to it.
She sits on the floor with it. She detaches the letter and reads it. She rips open the package. It's two halves of a cardboard cutout of a man in military uniform. She looks at it. She fits it together. She dismantles it. She takes it out to the utility room and comes back without it.
She goes to the kitchen and tidies/cleans.
She goes to the utility room and emerges with the cardboard cutout. She considers it. She places the top half and the legs against the settee.

Cup of tea.

She goes to the kitchen and makes a cup of tea. She gets out two cups but puts one back. She makes a bowl of cereal and sits at the kitchen table. She half turns from the cutout. She goes and gets the top half and plonks him in the seat opposite. She offers him some food.

Not hungry?

She puts a bowl and spoon out for him. She 'listens' to him and turns the TV over.
She realises she is wearing her pinny, goes and takes it off, plumps up her hair and sits back down.
She suddenly makes the noise and actions of a cat.
She does it again.
And again.

Pause.

She makes the action and noise of a microwave oven.
She does it again.
She goes and considers the legs, measuring them against her

own. She puts the legs away and reads a book.
She gets his top half and props him up on the settee, next to her,
gets the legs and puts them sticking out from the body.
She gently touches his hair, cleans a mark from his face.

God, David you don't take a great photo. You've got a certain
something, but this thing . . . It's as if your good features have
been flattened away, turning plain into plain ugly. Maybe it's
the plastic coating . . .

She goes and gets the polish and gives his top and bottom half a
polish.
She puts his slippers on him.
She gives him a hug.

I've another man in the house. Although you can't complain
because, technically, it's you.

It's not uncommon for women like me to have affairs. Home a
lot, a man calls, maybe a plumber or a TV repair man with a
moustache, a line of banter and a way with my Sky box. I'm
feeling vulnerable . . . one thing leads to another . . . *(she*
sighs) . . .

She makes him 'comfortable' by laying him down on the settee,
putting a cushion below his head. She gets him a drink. She goes
and gets him a blanket and puts it over him.

Forgot to take off your slippers.

She takes off his slippers.

And a towel, for the morning.

She goes and gets a towel and puts it next to the settee.

Like a hotel.

She tidies, quietly.

There's a storm brewing.

In the air. There's less of it. Less air. You always said I've got a sixth sense, which is superhuman, a bit like that tall bird with the big thighs and the gold hat. 'Wonderwoman'.

She goes to bed. She plays with the globe in her bedroom, spinning it.
She goes to sleep.
She gets up.
Donna is on a ledge, looking down.

– Oi!

She freezes.

– Oi! Careful.

I'm okay. Thank you. Goodnight.

– Oi! You're a bit close to the edge. I'm going to phone the fire brigade.

No need. I'm okay. Go back to doing whatever you were doing.

– What are you doing up here?

I'm going to jump. Just leave me alone.

– I would but if you jump and die and I'm up here at the same time what are the police going to think? They'll think lovers' tiff, he's pushed her, slap the cuffs on, prison. Me in prison. Marvellous.

Oooh, Christ.

– I'm too young for prison.

Christ, ooooh. It's high.

– I like heights.

Don't come near me.

– Do you like heights?

No.

– What you doing up here then?

Silence.

I don't want to die. I just want to do . . . something. If I step off I might be able to fly. I could fly around the car park and look down.

Beat.

Check my bike is safe.

He climbs up and sits near her.

– It's a great view.

I've been to see my boyfriend, Stephen, and my eye still hurts.

I was in the shop and in comes this gang of special needs students and one of them pokes me in the eye with a child-friendly thermometer. Mrs Field sent me home. Could hardly steer my bike. But I don't want to see my dad so I came here, to Stephen's, and I went up the stairs and I opened the door and he was in.

– That's good.

With my best friend Lucy. And they are . . . together.

– Aaaah. Not so good.

They didn't see me and I just started up the stairs again and went up and up and here I am. I don't know what to do.

– Has he got a car?

What?

– I could get a brick and smash his windows.

You'd do that?

– Like I was twelve again. Then run away.

It's that one, the blue one.

– If, right, I was to hold a brick above the place where his car is and just let go, technically it wouldn't be me doing the smashing but gravity. All I'd be doing is letting go.

I liked him.

– Yeah, he seems like a great bloke.

Beat.

What are you doing up here?

– Saving you. From gravity. What's your name?

Donna.

– David.

He holds out his hand. After a second, she shakes it.

– Do you come here often?

That's a terrible line.

– Do you?

Silence.

– Really, I'm up here counting seagulls. Well, seagull nests.
The council want to find out how many there are before they
take over the world. One day a seagull will be prime minister.
But it's not my proper job. Temporary, bit of cash like. I'm in
the Army. Well, I've joined up anyway. I'm going to be a
killing machine. Maybe I should have joined the fire brigade.

You're an action man.

– Yeah, if you look closely, just here, you can see the button
that moves my eyes from side to side.

She laughs.

– What do you do?

I work in Mothercare. Lots of pregnant women buying stuff they don't really need.

– You got any kids?

I haven't even got a boyfriend anymore.

It's getting cold.

– Yes, it is.

David takes off his jacket and puts it around her shoulders.

Thank you.

I wouldn't have stepped off, would I?

– Listen, why don't we discuss this over some chips? And maybe even a battered sausage. Before the seagulls get us.

Another day . . .

– We could go to the pub. Just for a bit.

What would my dad say about that?

– I don't care what your dad would say. I'm not taking your dad out on a date. He's not my type. So where do you want to go? *(Imitating her)* Nowhere noisy and but where there are some people so you don't get any funny ideas. The library?

Can't we just sit here and . . . enjoy? Enjoy the water.

They sit.

You're not enjoying yourself are you?

– It's okay.

My hands are cold.

He puts her hand in his pocket.

My feet are cold.

– Don't start.

They sit.

– Well, this is fun.

They sit.
David gets up.

– Can you skim stones? I'm an expert.

He picks up a stone and skims it.

– One, two, three . . . I've done six in the past. You do one.

What if I hit a duck?

She gets up and throws.

– You throw like a girl.

He shows her how to throw.

– Go on.

She throws.

– One, two, three, four, five, six . . . seven, eight. Bloody
hell.

He throws.

– What does your dad do?

Protects me.

– Is he bigger than me?

Yes.

– Have you got any brothers or sisters?

No, only child. Spoiled rotten. You'd never keep me in the
manner to which I am accustomed.

– Keeping you now am I?

I'm not marrying you.

– Can you scratch my back?

She does.

What did your last slave die of?

– Not scratching my back. Bit lower.

Another day . . .

A lovely day, all in all, wasn't it? Greatest day of a young girl's life. Turn up, walk, repeat special words with sincerity.

– I do.

Rings, kiss, about turn, pass Debbie Vaughan and her baby. Mistake. Sick.

– Projectile vomit.

A flash bulb goes off.

Don't keep on.

– Projectile fucking vomit.

I'll projectile vomit you in a minute if you don't stop whinging.

Flash bulb.

– Kids should not be allowed

Where?

– Anywhere. Especially not in a fucking church.

More flash bulbs.

It'll come out.

– You'll get it out?

I'm not doing it.

– Love, honour and obey Donna?

Dry cleaners, David?

Flash bulbs.

Wish my dad was here.

– Give him time. He'll come round.

You don't know him.

– I'll get to know him.

He thinks we're mad getting married after two months.

– He's right. You're bonkers.

And you're barmy.

Pause.

– Is it gonna rain? What does your sixth sense say Wonder-woman?

I think it's going to be a beautiful day. I feel fucking marvellous.

– I think my face is going to crack.

It's cos you're not used to smiling.

– Fuck you.

Stinky.

– Pig.

Donkey.

– Monkey.

Octopus.

– Worm.

Maggot.

– Slug.

Slug-fucker.

Our first real kiss. The one in front of the altar doesn't count, but this one . . .

A flurry of flash bulbs.

I love you David.

– I love you too my Wonderwoman.

They sit, watching the sea.

– Beautiful.

Yes, it is. I like the way the waves just keep on coming.

– I meant you.

Beat.

– You don't mind?

I've said.

You go away a lot with the job so . . .

– There's not many wives would put up with Porthcawl for a honeymoon. At least we won this.

He hands her the teddy bear.

– What you gonna call him?

Him?

– Him, her.

I don't believe in giving names to stuffed toys.

– You're a hard hearted cow.

They kiss.

There'll be plenty of time for us to go away together.

– Do you like to travel?

When I was working in Mothercare I would pass the station each day and outside the station they had this/

– I can't imagine life without you. We'll be together forever.

Beat.

– Promise?

They are in love, playful.

– Have you been eating Jammie Dodgers again?

Only the one.

– What's for tea?

I dunno? Bangers and mash?

– On a Friday?

I

– On a Friday Donna? Are you mad?

Well

– Friday is for fish Donna. We always have fish on a Friday Donna.

I thought, you know a change.

– It's Friday, Donna. Friday is no day to start changing things Donna. Maybe a change on a Monday, Donna, but changing things on a Friday, a fishy Friday, is insane.

Fish on a Friday, Saturday chips, Sunday lunch on a Sunday, Monday's curry, with what's left of the meat from the roast, Tuesday pasta, after the excesses of Monday, Wednesday Chinese, there's a special offer at the Bamboo Garden, Thursday spag bol as it's easy to heat up after you come in from football training, Friday . . .

– You're so organised. You'll make a great mum.

Plenty of time for that.

– You'll make the best mum in the world. You'll have a mug and on the side it'll say The Best Mum In The World.

You don't want me to lose my figure yet do you?

– I'll love you forever. Whatever shape you are.

And I'll love you forever. Unless you go bald.

– I'll love you forever. Unless you go bald.

I won't go bald. My mother wasn't bald.

One, two/

– Wait. Right. I'm ready.

One, two, three.

Donna makes the noise and actions of a cat. David makes the noise and actions of tinfoil.

– Got you.

No.

– I did.

One, two, three.

Donna makes the noise and actions of a microwave; David. a cat.

– Me again.

No. Cat kills tinfoil, tinfoil kills microwave, microwave kills cat. I win.

One, two/

– I've been posted.

– Donna, I've been posted.

– I'll see you in eight months, be over before you know it and we can do all the things we want to do. Together. A proper home, get out of this flat. A proper home, with a nursery . . .

– I've been posted.

Where?

– Norway.

Right.

– I'm sorry, won't always be like this.

No, no, of course. It'll give us a chance to save more.

– Four years and I'll get out. Get one of them cushy private security jobs. Maybe set up on my own.

A proper home.

– A proper home.

As they speak Donna takes Cardboard Dad and places him in a chair at the table. She gets objects from around the home and makes a 'Donna' opposite him.

And all the things that fill it. All the wonderful things. The big things, like a king-size bed and a washer-dryer and the small things.

– The tiny things.

Four years?

– That's all.

And our children will go to school?

– What?

It's important that children go to school.

– Yes, it is.

That's that then. That's a plan?

– That's a plan.

I've heard if a woman goes past twenty-eight then things start to shrivel up, inside.

– I don't know/

And men. Sperm become lazy.

– Donna!

Like Springer Spaniels. You get them when they're young and they're full of energy, a hundred miles an hour. A few years on and they're content to sit in front of the fire.

– Who wouldn't love you?

Four?

– We'll be a family.

And when the children are a bit older it's easier. You can do what you want, there's more time as they are in school and not schooled at home. How exciting! Norway. You'll need a hat.

– I love you so much.

I'm not against home schooling but there's no getting away from it. Your school is actually in your home.

– Our children will go to school.

Nina Simone's 'New Day' starts to play.

You ready to order now? Sir? Madam? Good choice. And to drink?

She laughs to herself.

Remember? At the barracks. The mess hall, done up all posh. Me sitting there with my chicken chasseur, you with your steak. It's smoky and I'm drinking cava, on comes this woman.

She rushes to the stairs.

This goddess. In red and she strides through the smoke and she sings that song and there's no hush but she doesn't mind the smoke and the noise and the people not paying attention and the laughing.

– I love you.

And I'm feeling good.

She touches Cardboard Dad's face.

She cuts straight through it, cuts through the smoke and the noise and chaos and by the second verse every man, woman and officer has their eyes clapped on her. Red. Dark. She's smokier than the smoke. She's redder than the red on the regiment banner. And I'm feeling good. I'm the one that's feeling good, never mind her. She's singing the song but it's me feeling good.

The song finishes.
She steps back.

Oh Donna get a fucking grip.

She rummages in a drawer, gets out a bit of paper and a pin and sticks them to Cardboard Dad's chest.

Noticeboard.

Pause.

Never thought I'd see the day when you were useful round the house.

You're useful now. You serve a purpose. Contributing. How does it feel?

So what is it, half hour of Loose Women or shall we tackle that washing?

(Singing) And I'm feeling good

She clears away dishes and tidies the flat.
The doorbell rings. Donna answers it. More shopping, Tesco.
She takes the shopping and puts it in the kitchen. She rifles
through the shopping, which is all own-brand goods, and gets out
a packet of Jammie Dodgers (originals, not Tesco brand), opens
them and eats two.
She takes the bill and sits on the settee. She gets out her
notebook. She makes a calculation and writes in the book. She
tears out the page and gets out a box. Out of the box she gets a
jar. She puts the piece of paper in the jar which is stuffed with
similar bits of paper.
She pours out a glass of wine. She drinks.

If I was to say to you 'present', what would you say? Hmm?

Pause.

That's right. Something small and simple. It's not as if we
knew them that well. He's a corporal or some such in David's
regiment and she's, she's German. Lotte. So I look on the list
and I'd been putting it off and, this is a word of advice, if you
are ever faced with a wedding present list get in early. All the
cheap stuff goes. I look on the list and the cheapest thing is
fifty-two pounds. Guess what it was?

Pause.

A George Foreman 'Lean, Mean Grilling Machine'. Have you
seen Lotte? Have you seen George Foreman? On the box he
looks like he shovels it away. I bet they never even unpacked it.
There must be a mountain of unopened George Foreman 'Lean,
Mean Grilling Machines' out there. They should recycle them
and make a . . . hospital or something. A hospital that deals
with overweight German people.

She gets out an anniversary card and a small present and puts them in front of Cardboard Dad. She pours a second glass.

You'd think they'd let you come back for special occasions and that. But no . . . some vows are non-flexible.

Everything in moderation. Watch the pennies and the pounds will . . . the pounds, the pounds will. They will. Normally I wouldn't but on occasions such as this you have to celebrate. Yes, it's better, isn't it?

To twelve years of wedded bliss. This is what I do David. For twelve years. Do you do the same?

Down the hatch.

She re-pours. She looks at the card.

Twelve years of wedded bliss. Or about four, if you count the actual time we've spent together. I was going to get dressed up. Put on a dress. But if we're not going out. Where would we go? There's nothing round here. It's barren. People scuttle round here, they don't walk. It's just apartments, retro chic, lifestyle choices. This is a lifestyle choice? To live on the edge of a town in a building where all the lines are straight? Where would we go? To a bar where all the lines are straight and all the people are bright and laugh too loudly? And you're not dressed up.

She sits and drinks her drink.

This is nice.

Silence. Drink.
Silence. Drink.

It is something to celebrate. Most couples. Twelve years. It's a long time. An achievement. I know you're not here a lot . . . but it's still a long time.

One day, I think, you'll answer me back.

Can I tell you a secret? I bought a red dress once.

My red dress. From Dorothy's. It cost two hundred pounds. Two hundred.

– How much!?

Fifty-six pounds. In the Sale of Sales .

– That's a sale?

Down from two hundred.

– Jesus. I said get yourself something nice but/

You do want me to look good at this do?

– I do but . . .

My feet are killing me.

– Give over.

These posh people. They have a . . . a frequency, don't they? A frequency all of their own.

Fa, fa, fa, fa . . . ha, fa, ha, fa

– Stop it.

It's like dogs. It's up here.

Fa, fa, fa, ha, fa

– Donna.

It's beyond our range.

– Evening Major.

This dress isn't . . . appropriate, is it? Is it too red?

– It's too . . . snug.

Fa, fa, fa, fa, fa. Love your dress darling. They *were* all the fashion, fa, fa. Can you breathe in that dress, fa, fa? You should have worn something a bit more . . . comfortable dear, fa, fffuh fa

Donna has to sit down.

You do seem a bit. . . Oh dear, David, David, oh cripes David, darling, she's fainted over the buffet.

Is she pregnant? Is that what it is? Is your wife pregnant David?

– No, she's just a bit . . .

What's twelve eh? It's nothing special. It's not silver or diamond. Paper? Glass? Stone? Cardboard?

Donna takes a drink.

Cardboard.

She takes a drink.

When was the last time we really talked about something? The day you were posted? The wedding? The hospital?

– We're always talking. Me and you.

This is serious.

– I'm a killing machine Donna.

We never talk.

– We're talking now.

Yes, thank you. I feel emotionally satisfied.

Pause.

I'm sorry, how's your wound?

– Another couple of inches to the left Donna and you'd be a widow.

Would I get a pension?

– You would.

We're insured?

– Army.

So if you died, I'd be rich?

– Rich enough.

Pause.

What would happen if I unplugged this?

– Don't!

Why not?

– It would cut all power to the TV/DVD combo and I'd have to ask one of those gorgeous nurses to bend over and plug it back in.

She laughs.

How long will you be

– A month, then three months recovery.

You're coming home?

– Some. There's a specialist rehabilitation centre just outside London.

Oh.

Pause.

And then you're home?

– Donna.

I just worry.

– I'm doing this for you. I was shot for you. For us. For our future.

I'm only thinking

– That's your trouble.

I was only

– Always were a thinker.

I think you'll find David we are all thinkers.

Pause.

You'll be home then. And we can start.

What?

– I see Iraq's kicking off again.

But you've been shot!

– Well spotted.

You're not seriously thinking of going back?

I thought, every cloud and that, that you'd come home and we could start. Start properly.

– I'm in hospital Donna.

You want to go back?

– I don't need this right now.

But/

– Is this what they call friendly fire?

We said. We planned things. Four years David.

– Getting shot at by your own side.

But David/

– Listen, Donna, let me get well and we'll talk. Properly, yes?

We have to talk.

– And we will. As soon as I'm better. Yes?

You promise?

– This has been a setback.

A setback! You call getting shot a setback?

I wouldn't call it a setback.

– It will set us back.

How long?

– I don't know. We'll talk. When I'm better.

No, I'd like to/

– I could have died.

Pause.

– I'll let you into a little secret Donna.

Pause.

– There's no white light. No tunnel. No angels Donna. It's the here and now Donna. When that bullet hit me. I thought, this is it. This is it. All I could think about is, this is it. Waiting for something, something to happen. And it never did. Until they pumped me so full of morphine I could have got off that stretcher and ran back to base. The secret is Donna there aren't any secrets. I could have died. We have to make the best of what we've got. That's the secret Donna, we have to deal with what is real, not live in some world of wishes.

– I'm doing this for us, for us to have a future together. This, I promise you, is my last tour of duty. When my commission ends this is it. But I'll serve my time Donna, set things up and then it's you and me.

I love you.

– From the moment I saw you on that ledge I loved you.

– You're here Donna, in my heart and I will take you wherever I go. Whatever danger I face, I face it knowing I'm doing it for us. Right? You will wait for me?

I'll wait for you and then we can start. My love.

She considers Cardboard Dad.

Does it go off do you think? Will it lose its fizz? Things, things go flat don't they? Lose their . . . pizzazz.

She pours a drink.
The music comes on again.

(*To Cardboard Dad*) What? What? Huh?

The music's volume increases.
She speaks to Cardboard Dad, drowned out by the music. She is animated – explaining things.
She picks him up, places him in different positions, finally putting him on the settee.
She sits, exhausted, on the floor next to him.
She touches his stomach.
She gets up.

Should throw this away. Do love a drop of cava though. Throw it away, yup? Shouldn't have more than a couple of glasses.

She looks at the bottle and goes to the sink.
She goes to pour away the drink.

– Don't.

Long pause.

– You've started so you might as well finish it.

– There's only a glass left.

– It's a waste.

– A waste of bubbles.

– In fact, I have a raging thirst on me. If you're not going to finish it I could have it. I am parched.

Donna hesitates and pours the rest of the cava down the sink.

You shouldn't be talking.

– You shouldn't be listening.

I don't fucking . . . Fuck

She tries to calm down.

– I don't take up a lot of space.

You can't stay, David would/

– It's up to you. You're in control.

Donna laughs.

– Donna?

– Can you take this pin out of my chest, it really hurts.

Another day . . .

Cup of tea?

Silence.

– Yes. I'd love a cup of tea.

Silence. She does not move.

– Kettle won't boil itself.

She gets up.

– Perhaps we can get a Chinese. I won't eat much. Get a bottle of wine. Watch a film. Love Actually is on later. Hugh Grant.

You can't speak. You are a piece of cardboard.

– You left me in the corner for a week. My legs are killing me.

It wasn't a week.

– You can't treat me like this.

You don't even look like David.

– I do. In reverse. A picture. Except I've got better hands.

She stares at him.

– Thought we could get a quilt out, cwtch up, watch Hugh Grant being prime minister.

She puts him in the corner.

– I must warn you I can't see the telly from here. At least put me behind the sofa.

Shut up.

– And it's a bit draughty here.

She opens the door and puts him out.
He knocks.

– Hello?

He continues to knock.

– Hello? Hello? Can I come in?

She opens the door. He falls flat on his face.

– I prefer to be the other way up. Can you turn me over?

She moves him with her foot.

– Give me a kick is it? That's charming.

She kneels.

– Just turn me over.

She does so.

– That's better. Can we go back to being on the sofa again?

She picks him up.

– If I was you I'd shut that door. Don't want your neighbours to see you holding a piece of cardboard.

She puts him on the settee.

– Thank you.

You're welcome.

– So are we going to watch Love Actually or not?

She leans forward and turns the TV on.

– That Hugh Grant is a cock, isn't he?

She laughs.

Another day . . .

They sit.

– What's your ideal dinner?

Lunch dinner or dinner dinner?

– Dinner.

Sunday lunch.

– Gravy?

She nods.

What do you like?

– I like . . . Mexican food.

Mexican?

– Little bits. Spicy.

Pause.

– If I could take you out, anywhere in the world, where would you eat?

I'd go to Italy. Pasta. Light, some wine.

– I'd like to go to Italy. Inside or outside?

Outside. The sun on my face.

– And eat a lot of pizza?

Pasta.

– Pizza, pasta, all the same eh?

It's not. What would you have?

– Something exotic. Lasagne.

It would taste a lot better in the sun than phoning for one.

– But we can phone for one? Cos to be honest Donna, I'm
starving.

Another day . . .

– If I threw this pasta against the wall it would stick.

She laughs.

– As they say in Italy, bon buffola bon bullala.

You're making that up.

– City Pizza is not bad.

Not as good as Italy.

– We could go.

We could?

– We can go anywhere.

Best stay in.

– You're just worried about being seen with me out. What would people say? People would say I'm two dimensional.

She laughs.

More wine?

Silence.

– Why don't we go for a walk?

Cos it's raining.

– Staying in all day watching stuff. Loose Women .

You watched it too.

– I can't turn it over. With which hand do I turn the TV over?

Silence.

– I'm bored.

I'm bored.

– I offered to take you to Italy.

We'd need to book.

– No, we wouldn't.

Another day . . .

– I wish I could have a shower.

We could try it.

– It'd never work.

What else do you wish you could do?

– I wish a lot of things. I wish I could hold you, see what your skin feels like. I wish we could go for a walk without worrying what people think. I wish we could go to Naples.

Naples?

– What do you wish?

I wish we could catch a plane. Or even a train. And it's the old days, like a film, the colours are different and there's matching luggage.

When I was working in Mothercare I would pass the station each day and outside the station they had this cutout picture of this happy teenager, maybe early twenties who was looking over her shoulder with a smile and a rucksack. I decided her name was Jane. I saw her every day and I thought I want to go inter-railing. On a train, round Europe. Me and Jane would not travel together but would bump into each other. Maybe in Rome. Or even Naples. A day in Mothercare and I'd forget about her. Till the next morning when Jane'd be there with her smile and her rucksack and her get up and go attitude.

– It's not so big, you know.

What?

– The world.

And you're not so flat.

– Why don't you do these things? Everything you mentioned is possible.

You can't just go. Things to do; washing, ironing, shopping.

– If you weren't doing these things you know what you could do? You could just go.

Another day . . .

They are lying down, next to each other. Looking up.

– When I was young I wanted to drive a submarine. Not a big one with nuclear warhead capabilities but a small one. In a fish tank and I could explore. But I never did. Do you remember your dreams? Some people don't.

I do. I dream about the stars. Looking up at the stars. The different shapes. Space. It's the furthest you can go isn't it?

– When you lie in a field, not in the city, and you can see the stars, there are thousands

Millions.

– of stars. Sometimes you see a shooting one.

You seen one?

– Lots.

I seen one once when I was with my dad. It was like magic.
We were lying on a hill, just gazing and all of a sudden . . . it
was so fast, shooting across the sky and he said:

– Make a wish Donna. But for the wish to come true you have
to believe, deep down in your soul, deep in your heart. Now,
make a wish my beautiful Donna.

– Did you make a wish?

Yes.

– You ever lose an eyelash?

Yes.

– Ever blown the candles out on a cake?

Yes.

– Cross your fingers and hope?

Yes.

– Cross your fingers and hope now. Go on. What do you want
to happen?

I wish . . . this is stupid.

– It's all right to dream.

But they don't come true. It's easy for you to say these things.

– When you were a little girl you must have had wishes, you must have wished you'd meet an exceedingly handsome man who is not dissimilar to the flat man lying next to you.

And we were blissfully happy.

– I wished I was married to Claudia Schiffer.

You can keep on wishing then can't you?

– Yes I can. The important thing is to keep on/

I get it.

Another day . . .

– Morning.

Morning. Did you sleep well?

– Yeah.

Donna gets up.

– Where you going?

Make a cup of tea.

– I wish I had a cup of tea.

Don't start.

She makes to go.

– One sugar.

You getting up?

– Could do with a hand.

She gets him up and props him against a chair.

– So what exciting thing are we going to do on this sunny day?

DVD? Internet shopping?

– Go down that little café. Croissants, coffee.

I think we should have breakfast here. There's a film on later. *(Pause)* Channel 5.

– I thought you meant cinema.

You've been to the cinema?

– Yeah, I'm recycled. In a former life I was a cutout of Sylvester Stallone.

She laughs.

– I fancy going out.

Won't get very far on your own.

– Not unless there's a strong wind.

She laughs.

– Today I am going to get you out of this flat.

No thanks.

– Or rather, make you go out of your own accord.

No thank you.

– How would you feel if I just left? Left you all alone? How would that be?

It would be quiet.

– And lonely. And dark.

I'm not going out. That's it.

He starts to make an annoying 'popping' noise.

– I can annoy you a lot. A lot.

He continues to make the noise.

– I'll call you names till you run out of the house and slam the door behind you.

I'm not leaving.

– Scaredy cat, scared of the outside world. Scared by the big bad world.

Am not.

– Are.

Not.

– I believe you are not woman enough to go outside. Scared. Chicken.

He makes chicken noises.

– I'm going out.

– I need some fresh air. It smells in here.

The door opens. Cardboard Dad stands at the door.

Don't, it's not fair.

– I need some fresh air.

Come in. Please.

Cardboard Dad starts to hum a tune.

Get in here.

She grabs him and pulls him inside.
He starts to gag. And again. And again.

I don't know what the fuck you are up to but whatever it is just stop it. Just leave.

– Not without you.

The door opens. He leans out.

– Have you seen this? It's amazing.

She moves closer.

– Bloody amazing.

She backs away.
He makes chicken noises.

– Amazing.

She comes closer.
He grabs hold of her.

– Hold on. Hold on tight.

The stage is transformed into the moon – made out of cardboard.

Jesus

– We're here.

We're

– You're the first woman on the moon.

Fucking hell.

She clings onto a rock for dear life.

– What do you think?

I only wanted to go inter-railing.

– If you're going to travel

So?

– So what?

So it's the fucking moon!

– Spiky.

There's nothing

– It's not every day you get taken to the moon.

Thank fuck.

– Your language is getting worse.

Fucking A. One minute I'm in the flat, the next

– You're the first woman on the moon.

I'm on the moon without so much as a cardigan. Jesus, where's my mobile? Where's my fucking mobile?

– There's no reception.

I can't breathe, I can't fucking breathe.

– Look Donna, look at the earth.

It's spinning.

– What can you see?

There's no air. I can't . . . I can't fucking breathe.

You're going to kill me. I can't breathe.

Donna sits, gets her breath back.

– And your time starts . . .

Donna puts her hand up.

– . . . now.

Donna waits with her hand up.

Can I go to the toilet?

– The exam has started.

But I need to go.

– Should have gone before.

But/

– But nothing.

It's not/

– What?

Nothing.

– You could have anything in that toilet. Crib sheets, hidden answers.

But you've just been in there dad.

– Hidden, Donna. Secret, difficult to see or find, in a place of concealment.

Please, I need to go.

– Should have thought of that earlier.

I can't think

– Fifty-six minutes remaining.

It hurts

– Silence in the exam room.

It really does

Donna puts her hand to her crotch. She is finding it harder to breathe.

– Hands on the table.

Please dad, it hurts.

– Fifty-five minutes to go. Hands where I can see them.

It really hurts.

– Donna Peters!

But dad.

– Mr Peters in school, young lady.

We're not in school dad, we're in the kitchen. I want to go to school. Why can't I go to school like the other kids?

– Hands on the table.

Donna puts her hands on her lap. She pisses herself.

– Donna! Donna! Donna! Look up Donna, look up!

I can't

She gasps as she looks up.
Donna freezes.

Fuck me.

– Beautiful, isn't it?

Donna and Cardboard Dad look at the Earth.

It looks so

Beat.

. . . small.

– You wouldn't believe it, room for six billion people. On that one rock.

It's spinning.

– At a thousand miles an hour. And travelling round the sun at 67,000 miles an hour. Everyone's spinning. Either going away or coming closer.

Take me home.

– Look at the earth Donna. Hold up your fingers Donna, yes, hold them up, you can hold it, pinch the earth between your fingers. That's all it is.

This isn't right.

– Can you see all the people, all the lives, past and present, all spinning, going about their business, all small and spinning?

I shouldn't be here.

– I'll let you into a little secret Donna.

Pause.

– There's no white light. No tunnel. No angels Donna. But it's more than the here and now Donna. We have to make the best of what's in front of us. That's the secret Donna, we *have* to live in a world of wishes, not just the here and now.

– Can you see all the lives Donna? Spinning, brief, we see them and then they are gone, out of sight forever.

One minute they are there, the next they are gone.

– Spinning out of sight.

With no time to say goodbye.

– There and gone.

What are you doing? You look different, stop sobbing, stop heaving, your face is all stretched and wrong. Dad?

Pause.

What? Say it. Say the words. Sob them out.

– I love her. Will always love her. I made a vow, a promise. In sickness and in health. For richer and for poorer, forsaking all others. It's just the two of us now Donna, I'm going to take special care of you.

After a while you stop crying and laugh. A little laugh, as though you were being silly. Make yourself busy. You never touched me again. Ever. Busying about, tidying things, folding things up. You open the bedside drawer and get a load of mum's knickers and you just stuff them in a carrier bag. You open the middle drawer, get her socks out and put them in a bag and then you opened the bottom drawer. *(Beat)* In it that single item covered in crêpe paper. So gently you pick it up and put it on the bed, unwrap it, its crinkliness revealing . . .

It's mum's bra dad.

– It's not her bra

It is.

– No, it's not. *(Beat)* It's underwear. Her sexy underwear.

Oh.

– She never wore them.

Never, ever?

– She saved them. Was saving them.

What for?

– She can wear them today. This is a special occasion.

You're going to bury mum in her sexy underwear?

Pause.

I want to go home.

– But don't you see?

I made a promise.

– Can't you see?

I made a promise.

– It's spinning Donna, each time it spins is another day.

A promise.

– It's there and then it's gone.

Take me home.

– Look how small it is.

I made a vow.

Pause.

They return to the living room.
They stand in silence.

Jesus. I need a drink.

Donna looks around the room.

Nothing's changed.

– Hasn't it?

What? Don't play games with me.

Jesus, fucking Christ. What the fuck am I . . . ? I should have put you in the recycling.

– It's not too late Donna.

What?

– You're only thirty.

Only thirty. What the fuck do you know? You've got all the answers have you?

– You have.

Don't get fucking clever with me.

– All I'm saying Donna is that it's up to you.

You're just like him and him and promise me this and promise me that and say it's up to you Donna and in the end it's never up to me. It's never up to me. It's up to you and him. I never asked to go to the moon for Christ's sake.

– You have to get out of this flat.

Beat.

I do go out. When David's here . . . we go to the beach. I, I like to walk and he likes to sit in the car. I sometimes take an umbrella.

But it's too windy, keeps turning the brolly out and in, out and in like a heaving chest. I give up on it. Plant it in the sand. Walk on. Wet. Thunder. Crack. Lightning. I turn to see the brolly in flames. In the rain. With no-one for miles. On a beach. I'm getting wet but I'm glad of that. David's in the car. He's waiting in the car for me while I go for a walk. Reading the paper. Has a flask of coffee.

He saves me a bit for when I get back, it warms me up. He waits and I walk, avoiding the lightning.

You know when you pass a mirror you look, don't you, instinctively. You look to see how you are looking, just a glance. When I look in a mirror I don't see me. I don't know who I see.

– I understand.

You don't. You're made of cardboard.

– You keep/

It's a trick. This planet is not spinning. It's not, it's a lie made up by you and people like you so we do things we shouldn't. Saying the world is spinning, time is moving, is just an excuse to do bad things to people.

– Well fuck you Donna.

What?

– Fuck you.

And fuck you.

– If that's what you think you might as well shove me in the recycling now.

I should do that.

– Go on, fold me up and put me out with the trash.

She gets up and goes towards him.

– Easy enough, I'm disposable.

You don't know what I want. You don't know anything about me.

– No?

She grabs hold of Cardboard Dad and folds him in half. She gets a green recycling bag and shoves him in. She opens the door and throws him out. She slams the door and lets it take her weight.
Lights down.

ACT 2

A typical day for Donna . . .
She enters from the utility room, dustpan and brush in hand.
She sweeps up a mound of debris on the floor and puts it in the bin.
She takes the dustpan and brush back out to the utility room and re-enters with the polish. She sprays a bit into the air and smells it. She polishes.
She goes to the kitchen area and puts on a pinny. She opens some beans and puts them in a pan and stirs. She puts the TV on. She presses play on the video player. An aerobics video comes on. She does some aerobics. She stirs the beans. She gets two cans and uses them as weights while doing the video. She stops. She takes off the pinny.
She goes to the bedroom and puts on a hoodie which is too big for her.
She returns to the living room and takes the radio, a cushion and a book on to the floor. She tunes in the radio. It's 'Classic FM'. She turns it up and reads a book while lying on her front. She rolls over on to her back and reads. On the radio Mendelssohn's 'Wedding March' comes on. It's followed by adverts, one for a Relaxation CD, and then the news. There is an item about supporting the troops in Afghanistan. She listens to it then turns off the radio.
She gets up and sits on the settee. She gets a pen and paper. She is unable to write the letter. She gives the teddy, bear which is on the settee, a hug.
She goes to the bedroom and looks at David's clothes. She smells them. She does the buttons up on a shirt. She puts on a dressing gown.
She goes to the kitchen and sits at the table for a while.
She goes to bed. While she is lying there she spins a globe which is at the head of the bed.

She gets up, puts her dressing gown on again, goes to the kitchen and makes a cup of tea. On the way she picks up a notebook from the living room. She does an inventory of food and makes a list of what is needed.

She turns on the computer and does an internet shop.

She puts the notebook back and notices the polish. She takes it to the utility room, giving a spay and sniff on the way.

She goes to the bedroom and takes off the dressing gown.

The doorbell.

She answers the door. It's the Tesco delivery man. She takes the shopping and puts it in the kitchen. She rifles through the shopping, which is all own-brand goods, and gets out a packet of Jammie Dodgers (originals, not Tesco brand), opens them and eats two.

She takes the bill and sits on the settee. She gets out her notebook. She makes a calculation and writes in the book. She tears out the page and gets out a box. Out of the box she gets a jar. She puts the piece of paper in the jar which is stuffed with similar bits of paper.

She enters from the utility room, dustpan and brush in hand. She is holding Cardboard Dad.

She puts him in the corner. His middle has been taped up. Donna goes and gets the polish and polishes. This lasts for a while.

– It was terrible.

Shushhh.

– I was scared.

What part of shushh don't you understand? You know the rules.

Silence.

– I kept on imagining what I might have been recycled into.

Beat.

– Bog roll. I could have ended up as bog roll.

Give me strength.

She picks up her box, opens it.

– What you doing?

Shush.

– What are you doing?

Beat.

I get, it's a

An allowance but that makes it sound a bit . . . mean. If I come in under with the shopping I save the difference.

– For how long?

Twelve years.

I put a chitty in with the amount saved and then when I go out I get the cash from the bank.

She shows him the cash. There are thousands of pounds in the box.

– That's a lot of differences.

– When was the last time you went out?

Quiet now.

– Are we going to the bank today to get the savings out?

– Are we? Or have you saved enough?

Be quiet!

Pause.

– It must be nice.

Look, I said we have rules. You are allowed in the flat if you just keep . . .

She puts her fingers to her lips.
But after a while . . .

What? What must be nice?

– To get wet.

– Closest I'll get is a damp sponge.

– Then I might get soggy.

– Nothing worse than feeling soggy.

– Funny that soggy is how you describe wet

– Not limp or damp or

Jesus.

– I'd just like to ask

A bit of peace and quiet.

Beat.

Just, for a bit. So I can think.

Pause.

– It takes two to tango Donna.

What does that mean?

– You know, just that there's two/

We are not tangoing.

– I know, it's just a saying.

Not an appropriate saying.

– No.

I'm not dancing.

– I'll shut up then.

Yes, silence.

Pause.

You can't just take someone to the moon.

And then expect them to do the washing up, or the ironing or whatever the fuck they are supposed to do.

It's not fucking fair.

– I was/

It's not fucking normal. I don't want to go to the moon, or
Jupiter or anywhere. I don't want to be astronaut girl Donna ,
I don't want to be funny Donna , I don't want to be top of the
class Donna , I don't want to be good-girl Donna .

Beat.

Can you understand that? Can you get that through that thin
skull of yours?

She calms down.

– Can we go out now?

(Erupts) No!

– Later?

Look, I/

– It's just you're in here all the time and I'd quite like to

Look, I'm not

– There's a lot more out there than in here.

You know that for a fact do you?

– For a bit maybe.

Look

Please check your tickets carefully. Tickets are non-refundable but may be exchanged at the discretion of the Box Office. Latecomers may be asked to wait for a suitable moment in the performance before taking their seats. Please note the use of photographic or recording equipment is not permitted in the auditorium. Please ensure that mobile phones, pagers and digital alarms are turned off.

Archwiliwch eich tocynnau yn ofalus os gwelwch yn dda. Nid yw'r tocynnau yn ad-daladwy ond fe ellir cyfnewid y tocynnau yn ôl ewyllys y Swyddfa Docynnau. Gellir gofyn i hwyrddyfodiaid aros am oediad addas yn y perfformiad cyn cymryd eu seddi. Nodwch os gwelwch yn dda nad oes hawl defnyddio offer ffotograffig neu recordio yn yr awditoriwm. Byddwch mor garedig â sicrhau bod unrhyw ffôn symudol, pager neu larwm ddigidol wedi ei droi bant.

Company Number/Rhif y Cwmni 06002090
Registered Charity Number/Rhif Elusen Cofrestredig 1118364

TICKET
TOCYN

Sherman Cymru
Senghennydd Road
Cardiff CF24 4YE
Ffordd Senghennydd
Caerdydd CF24 4YE

Box Office/Swyddfa Docynnau
029 2064 6900
Minicom 029 2064 6909
boxoffice@shermancymru.co.uk
www.shermancymru.co.uk

Sat 31 Oct 2009 7.30pm

Cardboard Dad

Venue 2   Unreserved Seating No.17

£12.00
Mr R Lloyd

– I'm not asking the earth.

Are you trying to

– I think, deep down, you'd like to go out.

Donna laughs.

– We could go together. I've always fancied going on a roller coaster. Not the log flume though. Too wet. And we could get some candy floss and do you know anywhere that still does donkey rides?

Jesus fucking Christ.

– It's good to get out Donna.

If you're trying to, you're succeeding

– All I'm saying it's good to get out.

You haven't got a fucking clue. How dare you, how dare you invade my home, make me/

– Donna?

David will be home and that's it and that's it. Together. And we'll do all the things we planned.

– You're sure?

Yes.

– If you were mine I wouldn't leave you.

What?

– We'd dance every day and I'd walk with you on the beach.

Shut up.

– I'd kiss your neck.

Shut

– And the back of ears. Just where you like it.

– And hold you close at night. Entwined. Not separate. No bit of your bed and bit of my bed. We'd make love every night.

– If you allow me

I can't.

She starts to search in the cupboards.

– A leap of faith Donna.

I took a vow.

– It's why you brought me back in.

She finds what she is looking for: a chef's blow torch. Donna moves towards Cardboard Dad.

I can't do this

– There's no such thing as normal, Donna.

It's easier

She lights the torch.

– No, it's harder

Easier

– No-one's normal Donna. On the outside maybe they look it but inside Donna, inside . . .

It's easier, easier all round. I'm sorry.

She comes closer.

Sorry.

– Donna?

It's easier

– You're in control, I know

Easier. Sorry

– Don't do it.

It's for the best

– I was thinking about you.

You were?

– I was.

About me?

– Jesus Christ Donna I'm pleading

There's no point

– If I had knees I'd be on them

Just like the rest

– I'm not.

Scream if you want to go faster

– No, Donna.

Round and round.

– It's not like that, I shouldn't have

No

– I was just trying to . . . Donna?

Sorry. I'm sorry.

– Donna? Donna? Donna? Donna? Donna?

She is about to burn him . . .

– Make a wish Donna. But for the wish to come true you have to believe, deep down in your soul, deep in your heart. Now, make a wish, my beautiful Donna.

Music starts up. It's the introduction to 'New Day'.
She lays down the torch and switches it off.
Donna melts into the music. She opens a kitchen cupboard door

and in it is a red dress. She takes off her clothes and puts on the
dress.
A single spotlight hits the darkened stage. There is the sound of
hubbub from an expectant crowd. Donna walks into the spotlight.
She is resplendent in her new red dress, red shoes and red lipstick.
The crowd applauds and settles down. She starts to sing:

Birds flying high
You know how I feel
Sun in the sky
You know how I feel
Reeds driftin' on by
You know how I feel
It's a new dawn
It's a new day
It's a new life
For me
And I'm feeling good

Fish in the sea
You know how I feel
River running free
You know how I feel
Blossom in the tree
You know how I feel
It's a new dawn
It's a new day
It's a new life
For me
And I'm feeling good

Dragonfly out in the sun you know what I mean, don't you
know
Butterflies all havin' fun you know what I mean
Sleep in peace when the day is done

And this old world is a new world
And a bold world
For me

Stars when you shine
You know how I feel
Scent of the pine
You know how I feel
Yeah freedom is mine
And I know how I feel
It's a new dawn
It's a new day
It's a new life

For me

And I'm feeling good

There is applause as Donna reaches out her hand. Cardboard Dad comes to life and takes her hand. He emerges, elegantly dressed in a tuxedo. His tape is now a cummerbund.
They dance together. At the end there is applause. The hubbub of the club returns as if there is now a dance on. They glide about the room. The music . . .
He moves around her and takes her in his arms. He kisses her neck, she melts.

– It's okay.

She turns.

– It's okay. Do you believe me? It's okay to enjoy the moon and the song and the kiss. I love you. Do you believe me?

They kiss.

He sweeps her off her feet and sets her down on the kitchen
table.
She goes to say something but he presses his finger to her lips.

– Barman. Drinks. What do you fancy?

Something with bubbles in it?

– Champagne.

A cork is popped and they drink champagne. They listen to the
music.

When I was a little girl me and my mum would pretend we were
in the party from the *Ferrero Rocher* advert. The one with the
ambassador. I'd be a princess or a countess or some such and
my mum would be my companion. And after we had drunk
champagne and had eaten a whole pyramid of *Ferrero Rocher*
the ambassador's apartment would turn into a disco and the
lights would swirl around the room and we would dance. We
made a glitter ball by covering a light bulb in tinfoil with holes
in it.

They watch the lights of the party.

And then mum would play the part of a prince or a count or
someone appropriate and he would declare his love and give
me the largest diamond ever mined. We used a marble.

Pause.

Am I talking too much?

– You don't talk enough.

He rests his head on her shoulder.

A real party, real champagne, real *Ferrero Rocher*, real diamonds, real glitter ball. I never thought this would be real, for me.

Cardboard Dad goes to give her a kiss.

I. I shouldn't. I can't. You know that I want to but I can't.

Beat.

They kiss. They kiss so passionately it turns into a dance, moving around the room until they land on the sofa.
They sit.
She puts her head in his lap. He strokes her hair.

– I love you.

And I love you.

– I've a present for you. Something small and simple.

A George Foreman 'Lean Mean Grilling Machine'?

– No. Just wait.

Cardboard Dad gets up and goes to the bedroom.
He emerges with a baby in swaddling clothes. She is transfixed.
She can hardly believe her eyes.
She stares at the baby.

Oh God, oh God, no, no, no. I never thought, I never thought, thank you, thank you, I never thought, I never dreamt, I dreamt but I never thought, thank you, thank you, thank you.

He hands her the baby.

Watch her head.

Hello.

She kisses the baby.
She smells the baby.

– Lucky she looks like you.

She's got your ears. We can always hide those.

Look at what we did.

She's wonderful.

– You'll make the best mum in the world.

I will?

– It's official.

Cardboard Dad gets out a mug which has the words 'The Best Mum in the World' printed on the side and gives it to her.

– What are you going to do Donna?

I

– Yes?

I

– You'll?

I'll take her to the park. Round the park, avoiding big dogs and teenagers on bikes. I'll nod to other mothers and be in their club, their special We've Given Birth Club. The We've Got A Life Club. And I'll be strict but not too strict and she will go to school. She won't be schooled at home. And she'll have friends and we spend time together and she plays soccer and I'm a soccer mom on the sidelines shouting her on, encouraging her. And when she's older we are best friends, we even go to Victoria's Secrets together.

– She's going to be busy.

She is.

– What's her name? How about Erica. Like Eric but for a girl.

No! Something pretty. Rachel.

– It's a lovely name.

With tears in her eyes, Donna laughs.

– What's it like to hold her?

Beat.

Like holding a crystal feather. Fragile but I fear she might float away.

Donna gets up with the baby. She kneels at her 'memory box' and opens it.
She gets out a picture.

That's your nanny. She's looking down on you.

She gets out a small, scruffy stuffed toy and shows it to the baby.
She gets out another picture.

And that's me. When I was young.

Cardboard Dad moves towards the utility room.

We're going to go inter-railing like Jane and I'll wear one of those baby carrying poncho things like the trendy mums wear and no one will ever guess I've been to the moon.

Cardboard Dad goes off, to the utility room.

I'm not gonna be buried in my sexy underwear.

I look good. I look like a Donna. Confident. Complete. Completed. Thorough, absolute, finished, having all the necessary parts.

You know what Rachel? I feel fucking marvellous.

BANG.

BANG.

BANG.

BANG.

BANG.

– Donna? Donna? Donna love. Are you in there? My key doesn't work.

– Donna? It's David, Donna.

BANG.

BANG.

BANG.

– Donna love? Is it locked? It's me, love, let me in. It's David. Donna?

She goes and lays the baby on the bed. She gets hold of the top half of Cardboard Dad. She searches for the legs. She finds them and puts him in the cupboard.

– Donna? You in there?

– Donna, it's me.

BANG.

BANG.

BANG.

– Donna. Let me in. Donna, it's me, David, Donna. Donna? Donna? It's David.

Donna unlocks the door. She stands back as it opens. David enters, dressed in uniform and carrying a kit bag.

– All right?

She steps back. He follows her into the room.

– This bag.

– My God, you look . . .

She wipes her hand across her lips, smearing her lipstick.

– Donna?

Hello. Hello. Yes, cup of tea?

– What?

Cup of tea?

– Don't I get a cwtch? I haven't seen you in seven months.

Yes, yes, I'm sorry, I'm just . . .

They hug. They part.

– I thought I'd surprise you. You look . . . you've dressed up.

Do you want something to eat?

– No.

Some soup? A bath? Shall I run you a bath?

– What's the matter?

Nothing.

Donna busies herself by making a cup of tea.
David collapses on the settee.

– That is the business. Oooh. Telly.

He switches on the TV with the remote.

– Loose Women is still on? Should have a programme called Loose Men . Wouldn't be allowed.

He watches TV. Donna watches him.

– Any chance of my slippers love?

She gets the slippers and hands them to him. He puts them on. He watches TV. Donna watches him.

– You been okay?

Yes. Fine. I've been fine.

Pause.

– So, what have you

Same, same, you know.

Pause.

– You look . . . stunning.

Thanks. You've lost weight. Have you lost weight?

Long, embarrassed pause.

I'd better get changed.

– I haven't seen that dress before.

I bought it

– Yes

Before. I wore it. Once.

– Right. I don't, yes, yes, I have it. New Year's Eve when we went to that restaurant – the one with the blue front. Well when I say New Year's Eve it was our New Year's Eve as it was really middle of January cos I couldn't . . . you wore it then.

No.

Pause.

– Anyway, you look nice.

– Don't get changed on my account.

– As you wore it

Pause.

Right, I'd better

– What?

Make something, do something. A drink?

– Look, just come and sit.

I don't want to sit down.

– I'm just saying it would be nice to relax with my beautiful wife.

Where is she?

– What?

Sorry, bad joke.

– You're on pins.

You know what? I'm a tad nervous.

– It's like someone has put 10p in you.

Pause.

– Why was the door locked?

Beat.

– Donna?

– Why don't you come and sit down. Here?

– So?

– The door?

Safety.

– It's not safe?

It's safer. There's degrees of safety. There's safe which is fine but then there's safer which is better.

– I swear

What?

– I could hear voices.

That's not a good thing.

– What?

Donna points to her head.

– No, in here when I was . . . it was locked.

I speak

– To?

To myself. Lots of people do it, doesn't mean I'm mad.

– I was worried.

Pause.

– Not holding out on me are you?

What?

– Haven't got yourself another man, a fancy man while I'm out fighting the good fight?

– I know a woman's got her needs.

He makes a grab for her playfully which she avoids.

– Maybe he's hiding?

Don't be stupid.

– In the bedroom?

No.

– The bathroom?

David, please we

– Got him in the wardrobe?

Don't be so

– I think I can hear him breathing.

He moves towards the wardrobe.

– Is he in there?

No.

– Oh, I think the lady doth protest too much.

No, just, sit down, you must be/

– Come out, come out wherever you are.

David don't, it's not funny.

He moves closer the wardrobe and put his hand on the handle.

– One, two . . .

David.

He opens the door.

– Three. My God.

Donna can't look.

– My God. *(Beat)* They sent it.

David pulls out Cardboard Dad and looks it over.

– Well I never. I thought it was a joke.

Donna sits.

– I signed a form, they asked us to sign a form as part of a new scheme thing where they send this cutout so loved ones wouldn't forget what we look like. Weird huh? We're always signing forms for this or that but I never thought . . . look there's two of us.

He stands next to Cardboard Dad.

– Like two peas in a pod.

Beat.

– What do you think?

– Donna?

Pause.

– So this fella been keeping you warm at night?

– He's had an accident.

– Get a bit rough with him did you?

– Been pretending you're getting a bit of Davey loving?

He starts to move Cardboard Dad about in a sexual manner, slowly then quickly.

He continues.

Put him

He continues.

Put him

He continues.

Careful.

He continues.

Put him

He continues.

Put him

He continues.

For fuck's sake put him down.

David freezes.
He puts Cardboard Dad down.

– Um, I

– I didn't

– You okay?

Pause.

– I'm sorry.

– Sorry I couldn't be home for our anniversary.

– It's okay, bit of a shock, should have called ahead.

– I don't mind Donna.

What?

– It's okay to get dressed up when I'm not here. In the afternoon, I don't mind.

Donna turns her back.
He goes to her and doesn't know whether to touch her or not.
He decides against it.

– Seven months is a long time Donna.

Twelve years.

– What? Yes. The anniversary. We'll celebrate, sorry I wasn't here for the day, mark it again, go out.

Beat.

– I've been looking forward to coming home.

He moves close to her and starts to kiss her neck.

David, don't. Please.

He moves away.

No, no, I want to, it's just, not the right time. Not the right time, bad timing.

– Oh. Right.

Not right now.

– It's just that, I've missed . . . normal things.

She goes over and picks up Cardboard Dad.

– Sorry I didn't get chance to get you a present.

He starts to unbutton his shirt, throws his tie on the settee. He goes towards the bedroom.

David!

– What?

Uh, sit and I'll bring you a cuppa. We have to talk.

He ignores her and walks into the bedroom.

– I need to get this uniform off.

He takes off his shirt and puts on a hoodie. From the pocket he pulls out a letter. He looks at it. From the other pocket he picks out another letter. He looks at his clothes. He checks the pockets. In each of them there is a letter. He puts the letters back.

As he is about to leave the bedroom he notices the baby.
He picks it up.
He carries it into the living room.

– What?

Beat.

– What Donna?

– What Donna?

David grabs hold of the baby and pulls it out of the swaddling clothes. The baby is made of cardboard.

– Donna?

She looks at the baby.
She is absolutely devastated.

– Donna?

She turns away.
He goes and embraces her.

– No harm done.

– Just a, a bit of

He picks up the 'Best Mum In The World' mug.

– nonsense.

Beat.

– Yes?

Beat.

– You okay?

– You had me worried there, when I went in and saw

He half laughs.

– Jesus I thought, I'm sure it wasn't a nine month tour.

He releases her.
She takes the cardboard baby and gently lays it on the table.

– How's about that cuppa you promised?

David plonks himself down on the settee. Donna picks up
Cardboard Dad and puts him back in the cupboard. David
switches on the television as Donna prepares a meal.
The doorbell rings.
She answers the door. It's the Tesco delivery man. She takes the
shopping and puts it in the kitchen. She rifles through the
shopping, which is all own-brand goods, and gets out a packet of
Jammie Dodgers (originals, not Tesco brand), opens them and
eats two.
She takes the bill and sits on the settee. She gets out her notebook.
She makes a calculation and writes in the book. She stops. She
closes the book and puts the box away.
She goes into the bedroom and changes her dress, emerging in
her comfy clothes.

– What's for tea?

Bangers and mash?

– On a Friday?

I

– On a Friday ? Are you mad?

Well

– Friday is for fish Donna. We always have fish on a Friday Donna.

I thought, you know a change.

– It's Friday Donna. Friday is no day to start changing things Donna. Maybe a change on a Monday Donna but changing things on a Friday, a fishy Friday, is insane.

Pause.

What was it like?

– Tough.

What did you/

– Look. Can we leave the Army talk for a bit?

Pause.

But we can talk?

– What?

Start to talk.

– Have you seen that new PC World? Big purple thing.

I've not been out much.

– Big thing, you can't miss it, behind Swan Street. Massive. They must have chucked that up. It's changing round here. Not like it was.

How does it feel?

Beat.

To be home at last?

I did have a bottle of cava but . . . we can plan now and get a home, a proper home and you're out of the Army and I'm not too old and in time/

– I meant to tell you.

What?

– It's a great opportunity

– Maybe a bigger house.

– More money.

– Too good an opportunity.

– They've offered me a new commission.

She stops, but is calm.

– I'm in line for promotion.

– Staff Sergeant Wilson. How does that sound?

– Aren't you pleased?

– I know but it's a promotion Donna. More money? For us.

You said you had a dream, start out on your own, a little firm of your own, a little gold mine. Private security.

– Economic forces Donna. The big boys have got it sown up. Since Iraq.

But

– Maybe five years ago but now . . .

- It's not realistic.

Beat.

– I know it'll take time to sink in but in four or five years . . .

She looks around her.

Five years

– And there's no need for you to work now, Donna.

Five

– I know I nag you about getting a new job. But only to get you out and about and meeting people but you don't need to work now and maybe you could always take up classes.

Cookery, needlework, computers for dummies?

– That type of thing.

Another tour?

– You don't mind?

You have to do what's best David.

– I knew

Do what's best for you David.

– You're one in a million Donna. You know that?

Beat.

– I love you, Wonderwoman.

Pause.

David?

– Yes?

How do I look?

– Fine, I/

Do I look like me?

– What?

Do I?

I need to know. Do I?

– Yes. Yes. You look just like you.

Pause.

David gets up.

– One, two, three

David makes the noise and actions of a cat.
Donna does not respond.
He does it again.
He makes the actions and noise of a microwave.
Donna does not respond.
David gets his jacket.

– I'll get us something. Something with bubbles in it. A bottle of cava.

– To celebrate.

He leaves, leaving the door open.
Donna approaches the door and stands there staring at the open space for a few seconds. She shuts the door.
Music: Nina Simone's 'New Day'.
She opens the cupboard and takes hold of Cardboard Dad.
They dance as she rests her head on his shoulder.
The door opens. David comes into the room.

– Sorry I forgot my/

Donna ignores him and continues to dance.
He walks into the room, picks up his wallet, never taking his eyes off Donna and Cardboard Dad as they dance. David leaves.
She finishes the dance, puts down Cardboard Dad, kisses her fingers and touches them to his lips.

She goes to the drawer and collects the box.
She leaves.

Blackout.

Dalier Sylw Publications

Y Cinio (Geraint Lewis)
Hunllef yng Nghymru Fydd
(Gareth Miles)
Epa yn y Parlwr Cefn (Siôn Eirian)
Wyneb yn Wyneb (Meic Povey)
"i" (Jim Cartwright – Welsh
trans. John Owen)
Fel Anifail (Meic Povey)
Croeso Nôl (Tony Marchant
– Welsh trans. John Owen)
Bonansa! (Meic Povey)
Tair (Meic Povey)

Sgript Cymru Publications

Diwedd y Byd / Yr Hen Blant
(Meic Povey)
Art and Guff (Catherine Treganna)
Crazy Gary's Mobile Disco
(Gary Owen)
Ysbryd Beca (Geraint Lewis)
Franco's Bastard (Dic Edwards)
Dosbarth (Geraint Lewis)
past away (Tracy Harris)
Indian Country (Meic Povey)
Diwrnod Dwynwen
(Fflur Dafydd, Angharad Devonald,
Angharad Elen, Meleri Wyn James,
Dafydd Llywelyn, Nia Wyn Roberts)
Ghost City (Gary Owen)
AMDANI! (Bethan Gwanas)
Community Writer 2001 - 2004
(Robert Evans, Michael Waters
and othersl)
Drws Arall i'r Coed (Gwyneth Glyn,
Eurgain Haf, Dyfrig Jones,
Caryl Lewis, Manon Wyn)
Crossings (Clare Duffy)
Life of Ryan... and Ronnie
(Meic Povey)
Cymru Fach (Wiliam Owen Roberts)
Orange (Alan Harris)

Hen Bobl Mewn Ceir (Meic Povey)
Aqua Nero (Meredydd Barker)
Buzz (Meredydd Barker)

Sherman Cymru Publications

Maes Terfyn (Gwyneth Glyn)
The Almond and The Seahorse
(Kaite O'Reilly)
Yr Argae (Conor McPherson –
Welsh trans. Wil Sam Jones)
Amgen:Broken (Gary Owen)
Ceisio'i Bywyd Hi (Martin Crimp
– Welsh trans. Owen Martell)

Available from:
Sherman Cymru,
Senghennydd Road,
Cardiff, CF24 4YE
029 2064 6901